AF131349

BOOK ANALYSIS

By Jessica Wheeler

The Left Hand of Darkness

BY URSULA K. LE GUIN

URSULA K. LE GUIN

AMERICAN AUTHOR

- **Born in California, USA, in 1929.**
- **Died in Oregon, USA, in 2018.**
- **Notable works:**
  - *The Dispossessed* (1974), novel
  - *Always Coming Home* (1985), novel
  - *Tales from Earthsea* (2001), short story collection

Ursula K. Le Guin was born in Berkeley, Northern California on 21 October 1929 to parents Theodora and Alfred Louis Kroeber. Both of her parents were academics and she therefore grew up in a home where education and learning were thoroughly encouraged. Le Guin obtained an MA in French from Columbia University in 1952 and was then awarded a grant which enabled her to undertake her doctorate and study in France. However, Le Guin met and married her husband Charles in 1953 and gave up her doctorate work. Le Guin and her husband went on to have two daughters and a son. She taught alongside her writing career and her duties as a mother, and gained much success over the course of her life. Le Guin initially struggled to have her work published when she began writing, but went on to win many awards and received much recognition for her published works and academic achievements.

THE LEFT HAND OF DARKNESS

SCIENCE FICTION NOVEL

- **Genre:** novel
- **Reference edition:** Le Guin, U. (2018) *The Left Hand of Darkness.* London: Orion Publishing Group Ltd.
- **1st edition:** 1969
- **Themes:** gender, communication, duty, warfare, honour, trust, loyalty and betrayal, desire, sexuality

Le Guin's novel was written and published as the second wave of feminism began to take hold all over the world. For this reason, much criticism of her work has centred on the fact that she chose to base her story around an androgynous race. The reason for this is that Le Guin wished to create a fictional world in which gender took a back seat in the social relations between individuals.

Le Guin's novel was seen as radical and groundbreaking in its style, and as a result of this she won two awards for the piece. *The Left Hand of Darkness* won both the Hugo and Nebula awards, which made Le Guin the second author to lay claim to this double achievement, and the first female author to have done so. Le Guin also managed, through this text, to break her way into the male-dominated world of science fictional writing.

SUMMARY

1.

The story opens with the speaker telling the reader that what they are about to read will be delivered as a story, although it is more of a report. The speaker is Genly Ai. His story begins with a description of his participation in a parade in Erhenrang, which is the capital city of Karhide on the planet Gethen. Ai describes the parade in detail, paying attention to the participants and their style of dress, the music played on various instruments, the weather, and the absence of any military. The parade ends at the newly built arch which has been erected at the port of Erhenrang, where King Argaven XV is to finish the arch by putting in the keystone. Ai has established a friendly relationship with Therem Harth rem ir Estraven, the King's prime minister, who invites him to dinner that evening. At dinner, Estraven tells Ai that he can no longer support his cause on the planet Gethen and act on his behalf with the King.

2.

The next chapter records a Gethen folk tale which supplements Ai's story.

3.

Ai has a meeting with the King. Just before he enters this meeting, Ai hears the news that Estraven has been exiled from Karhide. This news makes Ai nervous of his own fate. When Ai meets with King Argaven, he tells Ai that Estraven had in fact been advising him to refuse to meet with Ai. Argaven calls Estraven a traitor and warns Ai not to trust anyone. The King then urges Ai to state plainly what his business is. Ai tells Argaven that he has been sent by the Ekumen, a league of 83 planets who want to extend membership to Gethen. Ai explains to the King that "the Ekumen is not a Kingdom, but a co-ordinator, a clearinghouse for trade and knowledge" (p. 56) between human worlds. Despite this explanation, Argaven refuses the offer. King Argaven is obviously unnerved by the sexuality of other planets, which differs from that of Gethen. Ai tells him that the sexual androgyny which characterises Gethen is very unique and unseen on any other planet, but to Argaven a person who is permanently male or female is a perversion of sexuality.

4.

This chapter is another folk tale which tells of two men who sought answers from the Foretellers (the equivalent of fortune tellers on the planet of Gethen) and were not satisfied with the answers they were given.

5.

Ai travels to see the Foretellers, and on his journey he does much thinking about the Gethenian way of life. Ai asks the Foretellers if Gethen will join the Ekumen in the next five years. He is given a one word answer – yes.

6.

This chapter is narrated in Estraven's voice. He tells of the morning he received the news he had been exiled and the journey from Karhide that followed.

7.

This chapter is a report summary of an investigation into the sexual physiology of the Gethenians. It surmises that the Gethenians were an experiment in terms of sexuality, and also details the reproductive cycle on Gethen. This sexual cycle lasts 26 to 28 days, and it is on the 18th day that 'kemmer' begins. It is during this stage that the individuals take on male or female genitalia, thereby enabling reproduction.

8.

Ai narrates what he observed as he travelled around Karhide. He hears a broadcast that announces that the King is pregnant. Ai then decides that it is time to travel to Orgoreyn, another country on the planet of Gethen.

9.

This chapter contains another Karhidish tale.

10.

Ai and Estraven are reunited in Orgoreyn. The political officials in Orgoreyn question Ai about why the Ekumen want Gethen to join them. Ai notices that they are much more direct in Orgoreyn than in Karhide.

11.

This chapter contains entries from Estraven's diary. He talks of Genly Ai and of his ignorance of many of the Gethenian ways. Estraven records that the media in Orgoreyn is being heavily controlled and therefore news of Ai's presence and his mission is not being circulated properly. Estraven's diary entries make it clear that there is political manipulation going on behind the scenes in the setting of the novel and that Ai is being used as a tool.

12.

This chapter gives another supplementary folk tale.

13.

Ai is arrested in the middle of the night. He is drugged and brutally interrogated before being put into a truck with a number of other Gethenians. They are all naked, having had their clothes as well as their basic humanity stripped from them. One dies on the journey. This chapter shows the prisoners' compassion for each other and their attempts to support each other in a subtle and unspoken way. The prisoners are all taken to a labour camp. Ai falls ill and is left in the infirmary with a Gethenian named Asra who is slowly dying. Ai and Asra exchange stories of their worlds. Ai says that on his planet the inhabitants are in permanent kemmer. Asra asks if this is a place of reward or punishment. In response Ai asks which Gethen is. Asra replies that it is neither. He says it "is just the world, it's how it is. You get born into it and... things are as they are..." (p. 204). Asra dies a day or two later.

14.

Estraven rescues Ai from the labour camp. The two finally begin to understand each other. Estraven believes in Ai's mission.

15.

Estraven and Ai decide to travel back into Karhide. The journey will be long and difficult. Their friendship continues to deepen, as does their understanding of each other.

16.

This chapter is a return to Estraven's diary entries. In the main, the content details the pair's difficulties on their journey. However, towards the end of this chapter, Estraven explains that he is in kemmer, and therefore finding the desire he feels towards Ai difficult to control. He eventually explains this to Ai, and they discuss matters such as loneliness, gender equality and the difference between men and women in Ai's world.

17.

This chapter contains the 'Orgota Creation Myth'.

18.

Ai narrates this chapter and talks of the journey with Estraven over the ice in the past tense. He says that they travelled for over 50 days. Ai recalls the night that Estraven told him he was in kemmer. He says that sexual intercourse between them was not an option as it would have likely destroyed their friendship and made them alien to one another once more. He says the emotional closeness that they shared whilst on their journey was more important and sex would have taken away from this. Ai also says that he finally came to see Estraven as both a man and woman.

19.

The pair finally make it to the border. Ai gets a message to his ship telling them to land in Karhide. There are two guards on the Karhide side of the border armed with guns. Estraven makes a dash for the border but is gunned down and killed.

20.

Ai is arrested and later summoned by King Argaven. Ai's ship lands. Ai goes to visit Estraven's family, and he gives them the diaries that belonged to Estraven. Estraven's family ask Ai lots of questions about his journey across the ice with Estraven and about Ai's homeland.

CHARACTER STUDY

GENLY AI

Genly Ai is the novel's protagonist, and he narrates much of the story. Ai is a foreigner in Karhide. He comes from the country of Terra. Ai is a male, and in his static sexuality he differs from the inhabitants of Gethen. He has been sent on a mission to persuade the Gethenians to join the Ekumen. Genly Ai is observant and patient when it comes to learning the customs in Gethen – he appreciates that to them he is an outsider and he tries to learn their ways from genuine curiosity rather than just as a means of being accepted. Genly Ai is still reluctant to trust many, as he finds it hard to read and understand the other characters and their motives. Genly Ai believes wholeheartedly in his mission to persuade the Gethenians to join the Ekumen, as he thinks it will improve their quality of life. He comes across as a very genuine personality: he does not try to fool others or manipulate situations for his own gain. Genly Ai is a very vulnerable character in the story, for he is like a fish out of water and an outsider with no true allies (until the second half of the novel, when his relationship with Estraven develops). Genly Ai is brave in the face of his suffering in the later part of the text when he is arrested and treated brutally. He reaches the verge of death but somehow manages to regain the strength to survive and eventually succeed in his mission.

ESTRAVEN

Estraven's full name is Therem Harth rem ir Estraven, and when he is introduced in the first chapter of the novel he is the Prime Minister in Karhide. He is also presented as an ally to Genly Ai, as he is in the process of getting Ai an audience with the King. Ai later feels that Estraven is not genuine and has in fact betrayed him. Ai shares this sentiment with the King, who believes Estraven to be a traitor and has him exiled from Karhide with the threat of execution if he returns. Estraven proves himself to be loyal to Ai later in the story when he rescues him from the labour camp and travels with him across the ice to deliver him back to Karhide, thereby risking his life. Estraven remains in the role of protector towards Ai, and his loyalty is proven through his tragic death towards the end of the story. Estraven also proves himself to be truly patriotic, as his support for Ai's mission stems from the fact that he wants the best for his country and its citizens, and he sees that membership in the Ekumen could be a positive change. Estraven acts as a mentor towards Ai as he teaches him the Gethenian ways and helps him to understand the culture. As with Ai, it initially takes him some time to be patient with the ignorance which stems from the cultural differences. In the end, Estraven forms a close and beautifully touching bond with Ai that transcends their differences.

KING ARGAVEN

King Argaven is hostile towards Genly Ai; not just because he is a foreigner in Karhide, but also because the King believes that this outsider may pose a threat to his power. Argaven's character is formulated on the basis of his position as monarch. His power defines him. He is pompous and rude and does not put the needs and welfare of his country and countrymen before himself, as if he did he would be more open to Ai's proposals. King Argaven is said to become pregnant about halfway through the novel, but he later loses his child. By the end of the novel, it can be specu-lated that this loss has impacted his character. He seems less hostile towards Ai, not as a result of having obtained more trust in him and his mission, but more because he seems deflated by the death of his child and the grief that weighs on him as a result.

ANALYSIS

SEX AND GENDER

The humans on the planet Gethen do not have a fixed biological sex, and gender roles on this planet are therefore also fluid. Childbearing is something that all Gethenians can do thanks to their unique biological constitution. This in itself has a huge effect on the structure of gender roles. When Ai is asked to explain the basic social differences between men and women on his home planet, he struggles. Estraven asks Ai if men and women differ greatly in "mind behavior" (p. 255) and if women are mentally inferior. Ai's answer outlines that in a gendered society, women do not tend to pursue jobs in mathematics, music or in abstract thinking, but this is not because their intelligence does not match that of their male counterparts. He explains to Estraven that on the planet Terra, a person's sex is the most important factor in their life: "it determines one's expectations, activities, outlook, ethics, manners – almost everything" and it is "extremely difficult to separate the innate differences from the learned ones" (*ibid.*).

Ai's description of gender is representative of what is found in current Western societies, as well as many others. The gender structure in Gethen, however, is a complete subversion of this. Le Guin has chosen to challenge the gender norms that existed in her environment, and that still last into the modern day, through her construction of gender on the planet Gethen. By juxtaposing this inverse construction of gender and sexuality against the norm which many readers would be familiar with, Le Guin very effectively highlights the way in which gender norms are mistakenly believed to be natural and innate rather than socially formatted. Le Guin demonstrates the blurred relationship between gender roles and biological sex, and the way that these things order society and inform the way individuals interact and understand each other.

DESIRE

Le Guin represents desire as a cycle in *The Left Hand of Darkness.* Chapter Seven gives a detailed explanation of the sexual cycle of the Gethenians, although the social rules attached seem to vary ever so slightly in some countries. The cycle lasts for 26 to 28 days, but the individual only experiences sexual desire for approximately six of these days. During the first 22 days, each Gethenian is in a state of somer, or sexual latency, where they do not experience sexual desire and do not possess either male or female genitalia. During this phase, sexuality and desire do not factor much in the lives of the individuals on the planet of Gethen. By the 22nd day of the cycle, kemmer begins and the sexual impulse kicks in with force, consequently "controlling the entire personality, subjecting all other drives to its imperative" (p. 112). The next few days of the cycle are defined by the search for another individual in kemmer to pair with, and desire is enhanced once a partner is found. This extreme desire is what gives rise to the individuals taking on either male or female genitalia in order to copulate. Individuals have no choice in the sexual role which they take on, and they shed this role after copulation has occurred unless they are in the female role and they become pregnant.

Genly Ai explains that on his planet, individuals are in constant kemmer – they are perpetually open to sexual experiences and feelings of desire for others. Estraven observes that the kemmer that Ai experiences is a "strange low-grade sort of desire" (p. 253) compared to that which the Gethenians are used to, as his is spread out over every day of the year. This is perhaps a curious way of considering the sort of desire that humans belonging to a culture such as Ai's experience. It could be argued that these individuals also go through cycles of sexual desire versus sexual inactivity, and to varying degrees. Desire may not be as structurally regulated amongst humans on Terra, or the Western society that this planet potentially represents, but neither is it evenly sustained as Estraven's comment suggests. Human desire, as it is experienced in cultures across the earth, ebbs and flows with differing strength and depends largely on the individuals who experience it and those they feel it for. As with the theme of gender and sexuality, this is one which is much more complex in the real world than in the fictional world that Le Guin has created, and her simplification of sexual desire in *The Left Hand of Darkness* therefore serves to highlight the many ways this phenomenon affects societies.

SCIENCE FICTION

The Left Hand of Darkness is a work of science fiction. This genre is characterised by a deviation from the norm and a call to readers to acknowledge the vast power and possibilities enabled by advances in science and technology. Science fiction novels are mainly set in alternative worlds and contain plots that stretch the bounds of the imagination. They commonly feature things such as alien life forms, space travel, time travel or the ascension to power of robots; areas which lie beyond the bounds of actual knowledge. Science fiction, as a genre, deals with all that is possible rather than what is known. As the name suggests, science features as a main theme in this genre, and it is a means of questioning the limits of what is possible. As the report on Gethenian sexuality in Chapter Seven details, the humans on Gethen are understood to have been some sort of scientific experiment in sexuality. The facts of how this type of experiment was carried out are overlooked as the emphasis lies on the question of whether such scientific advancements as this could be possible. This is the case with much science fiction writing.

Solid facts or details become irrelevant in the face of the larger picture – the alternative worlds that the imagination creates within the pages of a novel, and the suggestion that these imagined worlds may become a reality in the future.

As science and technology began to make advancements in the 18th and 19th centuries, writers began to express their wonder at the possibilities for the future through this genre of literature. Mary Shelley's *Frankenstein* (1818) is an example of an early science fiction novel. However, science fiction does not only detail or imagine possibilities for the future; it also thoroughly questions the ethical repercussions of the continuous advancements in science and technology. Le Guin raises the question numerous times throughout the novel of which form of sexuality is better, and whether a sexual cycle such as that experienced by the Gethenians is a blessing or a curse. Le Guin not only suggests that science has the capacity to one day effect changes such as these to the biological sex and sexual experiences of the human race, but she also asks the reader to think about the further effects that this could have on society and the quality of human life. In this way, Le Guin demonstrates the value of the science fiction genre – the power to imagine and question the possibilities for our future reality.

FURTHER REFLECTION

SOME QUESTIONS TO THINK ABOUT...

- In Chapter 13, Asra asks Ai if a world where humans are constantly in a state of kemmer is a reward or a punishment. What would be your answer to Asra's question?
- Why do you think Ai and Estraven avoided entering into a sexual relationship while they were journeying to Karhide? Do you think the reason is to do with sexual attraction?
- Do you think the chapters that contain Gethenian myths and folk tales support the story and the plot? If so, how? If not, why not?
- There is more than one narrative voice in the novel. How does this affect the story?
- Do you think that the gender stereotypes that Genly Ai would be used to on his own planet (like those that exist in current Western society) impact his ability to understand the androgyny that exists on Gethen?
- Which planet would you rather live on, Gethen or Earth? Explain why.

- What is the main message that you think Le Guin is trying to deliver through this text?
- The androgynous nature of the Gethenians is slowly revealed to the reader rather than being laid out in full from the beginning. Do you think this was a good choice? Why, or why not?

We want to hear from you!
Leave a comment on your online library
and share your favourite books on social media!

FURTHER READING

REFERENCE EDITION

- Le Guin, U. (2018) *The Left Hand of Darkness.* London: Orion Publishing Group Ltd.

www.brightsummaries.com

Ebook EAN: 9782808019729

Paperback EAN: 9782808019736

Legal Deposit: D/2019/12603/153

Cover: © Primento

Digital conception by Primento, the digital partner of
publishers.